21.109

OAKWOOD COMPREHENSIVE
Property of
SCHOOL LIBRARY

D0272506

The Steam Engine

A Breakthrough in Energy

RICHARD TAMES

Heinemann
LIBRARY

First published in Great Britain by Heinemann Library
Halley Court, Jordan Hill, Oxford OX2 8EJ
a division of Reed Educational & Professional Publishing Ltd.
Heinemann is a registered trademark of Reed Educational & Professional Publishing Ltd.

OXFORD FLORENCE PRAGUE MADRID ATHENS MELBOURNE AUCKLAND
KUALA LUMPUR SINGAPORE TOKYO IBADAN NAIROBI KAMPALA JOHANNESBURG
GABORONE PORTSMOUTH NH (USA) CHICAGO MEXICO CITY SAO PAOLO

© Reed Educational & Professional Publishing Ltd 1998
The moral right of the proprietor has been asserted.

All rights reserved. No part of this publication may be reproduced, stored in a retrieval system, or transmitted
in any form or by any means, electronic, mechanical, photocopying, recording, or otherwise without either the
prior written permission of the Publishers or a licence permitting restricted copying in the United Kingdom
issued by the Copyright Licensing Agency Ltd, 90 Tottenham Court Road, London W1P 0LP.

Designed by Jim Evoy
Illustrations by Jeff Edwards, Oxford Illustrators
Printed in Hong Kong / China

02 01 00 99 98
10 9 8 7 6 5 4 3 2 1

ISBN 0 431 06880 1

British Library Cataloguing in Publication Data
Tames, Richard, 1946–
The steam engine: a breakthrough in technology. - (Turning points in history)
1. Steam-engines - History - Juvenile literature
2. Power (Mechanics) - History - Juvenile literature
I. Title
621.1'09.

Acknowledgements
The Publishers would like to thank the following for permission to reproduce photographs:
BEAMISH, The North of England Open Air Museum, p.29; Birmingham Public Library, p.11;
Guildhall Library, p.5; Hulton Deutch, pp. 19, 21; London Transport Museum, p.23;
Mary Evans Picture Library, p.6; National Maritime Museum, p.18; Rural History Centre, p.25;
Science and Society Picture Library, pp.7, 8, 9, 10, 12, 14, 15, 16, 20, 27, 28;
St Brides Printing Library, p.13; Thomas Cook, p.22.

Cover photograph: Mary Evans Picture Library

Our thanks to Jane Shuter for her help in the preparation of this book.

Every effort has been made to contact copyright holders of any material reproduced in this book. Any
omissions will be rectified in subsequent printings if notice is given to the Publisher.

Some words are shown in bold, **like this**. You can find out what they mean
by looking in the glossary.

Contents

Energy use: breaking the barrier

For most of human history people have had to rely on the power of their own muscles, wind or water for moving and making things. The steam engine created a new world in which people could produce more, build bigger and travel faster than ever before. Steam was the energy that powered the **Industrial Revolution** (1750–1850). This is the name given to the great changes that took place in how and where things were made – from hand-made goods produced at home, often in rural areas, to machine-made goods produced in factories, usually in towns.

From Stonehenge to St Peter's

Stonehenge is a huge stone circle. It was built around 2000 BC. The largest of the stones weighed up to 50 tonnes, and they were transported from about 30 km away. Each stone would have needed 500 men to drag it on rollers, with another 100 men to move the rollers from the back to the front and to stop the stone wandering sideways. It would have taken a year for 600 people to move each stone, and hundreds more people to grow the labourers' food, chop trees for rollers and plait leather ropes.

In 1586, 3500 years after Stonehenge was built, a stone column weighing 327 tonnes was moved a few hundred metres to St Peter's, in Rome. By then **pulleys** and **capstans** had been invented, improving the efficiency of simple muscle power. Even so, it took 800 men and 140 horses to get the job done under the watchful eye of an executioner!

Using labour on a large scale needs organization, and space. This picture shows the manpower needed to move a stone column a few hundred metres to St Peter's in Rome in 1586.

4

Steam-powered machinery, however, would make it possible for a single man to move such a load in minutes without even breaking into a sweat.

Water and wind

The ancient Chinese, the Greeks and the Romans all used water-mills. They used the power of a flowing stream, usually to turn mill-stones to grind grain into flour. The power provided by water was free for the taking but unreliable, as it could be affected by freezing, flood or drought. And, of course, the mill had to be where there was water.

The waterwheel at London Bridge was used from 1582 to 1822 to pump water to the city's houses.

The windmill was invented in Asia in AD 650. By 1100, Europeans were using windmills, mainly for grinding grain, but also for sawing wood, pumping water and ventilating mines. Wind, like water, was free but unreliable.

But steam engines were unaffected by the weather. They could run continuously, wherever they were needed. All they needed was the means to create steam.

On the hoof

Until steam-powered **locomotives** were invented, people could only travel as fast as the horses they were using could go, which was up to 60 kph for short bursts, but only 12 kph for long journeys. In Roman times the best journey time from Rome to London was about ten days. In 1834, when Sir Robert Peel had to go from Rome to London as fast as possible because he had just become prime minister, the journey took just as long. However, twenty years later he could have travelled as fast as a race-horse going flat out – for hour after hour.

Triumph and tragedy

A great event

Built to link one of Britain's busiest ports with one of its greatest industrial cities, the Liverpool and Manchester Railway was hailed as the greatest engineering project since the building of the pyramids of ancient Egypt. Engineer George Stephenson's 50 km line drove through great cuttings, along embankments, across a treacherous bog and even over a canal.

The Olive Mount cutting – one of the engineering wonders of the Liverpool to Manchester route.

The presence of the Duke of Wellington, who was prime minister, as well as foreign dignitaries and leading politicians, like Huskisson, the minister for trade, showed that the opening of this railway was seen at the time to be of historic importance.

The coming of the world's first steam-powered railway – ready to carry both passengers and **freight** – marked a triumph of technology. Although the event was overshadowed by the tragedy of the world's first death in a railway accident, the railways were here to stay.

In a daring attempt to get the injured Huskisson to a doctor, Stephenson pushed the locomotive to 80 kph – twice its previous top speed – showing just what steam could do.

MANCHESTER GUARDIAN, 18 SEPTEMBER 1830

The opening of the Liverpool and Manchester Railway took place on Wednesday last; and, until the proceedings were clouded by a lamentable accident, it was a very splendid and imposing ceremony. At half-past nine the gorgeous carriage, destined for the Duke of Wellington appeared. In the carriage with his Grace we observed Prince Esterhazy; the Russian Ambassador; Lord Stanley and the Rt Hon William Huskisson. Countless hundreds waved their hats to cheer. The engines went forward with arrow-like swiftness, twenty-four miles an hour became the maximum of the speed. At Parkfield, seventeen miles from Liverpool, the engines stopped to take in a fresh supply of fuel. Here several gentlemen descended from the different carriages. Among them was Mr Huskisson. The Duke extended his hand, which Mr Huskisson advanced to take. Sounds announced the approach of the *Rocket* engine, on the opposite rail; a cry of danger was instantly raised. The unfortunate gentleman missed his footing and the *Rocket* coming up at the instant, went over his leg and thigh, and fractured them in a most dreadful manner.

As Henry Booth, treasurer of the Railway, noted, the most basic ideas of time and space had changed forever; *'What was quick is now slow; what was distant is now near.'*

The grand opening of the Liverpool and Manchester railway, 1830.

Was steam power really new?

Steam

People had understood for a long time how steam could make things move. But they had not put this knowledge to practical use before. Hero of Alexandria, a Greek who lived in Egypt around AD 100, invented a basic steam engine. It was a **sphere** in which water was boiled. The boiling water made steam, which came out of two angled jets on opposite sides of the sphere, making it turn. In theory this could have been used to drive a machine, but in practice it was regarded as just an amusing toy. There were plenty of slaves to do any work, so there was little interest in labour-saving technology.

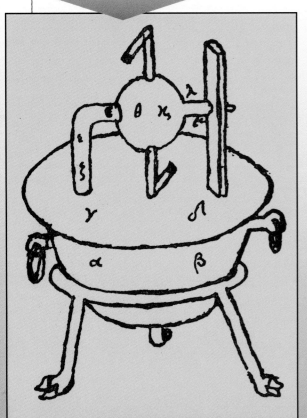

Hero of Alexandria's steam-engine

Atmospheric pressure

In 1654, German scientist Otto von Guericke proved the existence of **atmospheric pressure**. By pumping the air out of a **cylinder** to create a **vacuum** in front of a **piston**, he showed that air pressure would move the piston along the cylinder, even though a team of men pulling on a rope attached to it tried to hold it back.

Putting them together

In 1690, Frenchman, Denis Papin, made a simple engine using atmospheric pressure to move it along. Water was heated underneath a piston in a brass cylinder to make steam. As the steam expanded it pushed the piston to the top of the cylinder, where it was held by a catch. When the heat was taken away, the steam **condensed** back into water, creating a partial vacuum.

When the catch was released atmospheric pressure forced the piston down with enough force to lift a 30 kg weight.

A practical use

In 1698, English military engineer, Thomas Savery, adapted Papin's device to make a pump for pumping water out of mines. Flooding problems had prevented miners from digging deep underground. A practical pump greatly increased the amount of minerals which could be worked. Devon blacksmith, Thomas Newcomen, built an improved steam pump at a coal mine near Dudley, Staffordshire in 1712. It produced 12 strokes a minute, each stroke lifting 10 gallons of water. Newcomen engines were widely used in mines for the next 60 years.

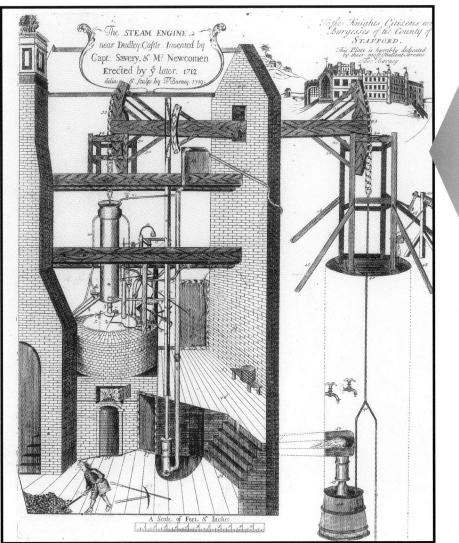

The Newcomen engine at Dudley

James Watt

An educated man

Unlike many of the inventors who made the **Industrial Revolution** possible, James Watt (1736–1819) was educated as well as practical. He was as interested in the scientific principles and ideas behind steam power, as in making the machinery work. Born in Greenock, Scotland, he trained in London as a maker of scientific instruments and was employed as a technician at Glasgow University.

Saving energy

In 1764, Watt was asked to repair a model of a Newcomen engine. He saw that while it worked well, it wasted a lot of fuel. He realized that it was creating the **vacuum** that wasted fuel, so he designed an engine that did not rely on **atmospheric pressure**. Watt's design, **patented** in 1769, used less than a third as much coal as a Newcomen engine. It worked faster and was much quieter too.

A productive partnership

In 1774, Watt joined forces with Matthew Boulton, whose metalworking workshop at Soho in Birmingham was one of the most advanced in Britain. Boulton was a brilliant businessman, skilled at organizing finance and workers and seeing new opportunities.

A Boulton and Watt engine with 'sun and moon' gearing system to convert pumping action into rotary motion.

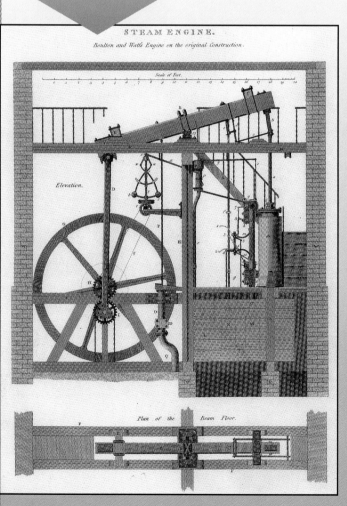

STEAM ENGINE.

Boulton and Watt's Engine on the original Construction.

He encouraged Watt to make further inventions, such as a system of gears to change the up-and-down motion of the steam-powered pump to a rotary (circular) motion to drive machines in factories.

The Boulton and Watt partnership helped to build nearly 500 steam engines, about half of all the engines in use in Britain in 1800. Watt also invented the notion of **horsepower** to measure outputs of energy. The unit of heat known as a **watt** is named in his honour.

Not just for coal mines

Cornwall was rich in copper, tin and lead, but not coal. This made Newcomen engines expensive to operate, as the coal had to be brought in from a distance. The first Watt engine, using far less fuel, was eagerly installed in 1777, when there were 75 Newcomen engines at work in Cornish mines. By 1783, there was only one Newcomen engine left in action there.

As well as the profit they made on selling their engines, Boulton and Watt also received a **royalty** equal to one third of the cost of the fuel they saved.

Matthew Boulton's metalware works at Soho, Birmingham

Industry adopts steam

The first industry to use steam engines to power every major stage of production was the cotton cloth industry.

King cotton

Machines powered by human hands or running water already existed for spinning cotton into yarn.

• By the 1820s, machines for both spinning and weaving yarn into cloth were powered by steam.

• By the 1830s, a single spinner could produce as much yarn in a day as her grandmother could have done in a year. One 100-horsepower machine could drive 50,000 spindles at once, producing 200,000 km of cotton thread every 24 hours – enough to go right round the Earth five times!

• By 1810, cotton had overtaken wool as Britain's biggest industry. Cotton items lasted longer than woollen ones. They were cheaper and easier to wash and so more hygienic to wear. Cotton cloth was also widely used for book-binding, bedding and in upholstery. So steam power affected everyone's lives by making cotton goods freely available.

By the 1830s cotton goods accounted for half of all Britain' s **exports.** British-made cottons were so cheap that even in India, where some of Britain's raw cotton came from, British exports destroyed the market for the local product. Even though the people making Indian cloth by hand at home lived in poverty, their cloth was still more expensive than British machine-made cotton.

Female and child labour in a cotton factory, 1835. The illustrator shows clean, calm conditions. In fact the air was often choking with cotton dust stirred up by fast moving machines which made a deafening noise.

Printing

Although there were machines to make the cloth, it was still printed by hand, so a bottleneck occurred at this stage. This was solved around 1785 by replacing the traditional block method (which printed one section at a time) with a **cylinder** which could print continuously. This made printing cloth a hundred times faster than it had been.

The Times printing press of 1814 could make 1100 impressions an hour. Hand-operated presses were immediately discarded.

Such a machine could be adapted for printing newspapers and books. In 1814, *The Times* became the first newspaper in the world to be printed on a steam-powered press. Designed by a German **immigrant**, Friedrich Koenig, it was four times as fast as hand-printing. By the 1850s, giant

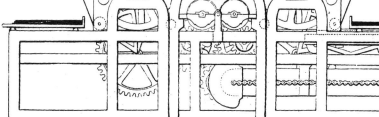

American presses could print 20,000 **impressions** an hour. By making newspapers and books much cheaper, steam-powered printing helped to encourage reading, and new ideas could be spread more easily.

British slavery

Women and children did much of the work. They had smaller, more agile hands than men. They could also be paid less! In 1824, journalist William Cobbett thundered against their working conditions, '*Slaves in the West Indies are better off than the slaves in these manufactories. In the cotton-spinning work, these creatures are kept, 14 hours in each day, locked up, summer and winter, in a heat of from 80–84F.*' Tired workers were also prone to terrible injuries from the machines, which had no safety guards at all.

Steam on roads and rails

Was steam always better?

In 1770, a French soldier, Nicolas Cugnot, invented a steam-powered carriage for hauling **artillery**. It was very slow and hard to steer. After it crashed into a tree he gave up his experiments. Steam-powered carriages were used on roads in England in the 1830s but they were slow, unreliable and so heavy that they damaged the road surface. They could not compete with trains running on rails or horse-drawn carriages on roads. They were never widely used.

Using rails

From about 1400 onwards wooden rails had been used to carry hand-pushed carts in German mines. By the eighteenth century, mines in northern England were using horse-drawn wagons to haul coal along longer-lasting metal rails to riverside loading-points.

Trevithick's locomotives

Mine owners experimented with fixed steam engines to haul wagons along on ropes. From this it was a short step to devising a **locomotive** – an engine that would develop enough power to move itself along and haul a load. The leading pioneer in this field was Cornish mining engineer Richard Trevithick (1771–1833), who built a locomotive for the Coalbrookdale Ironworks in Staffordshire in 1803.

Cugnot's steam carriage for pulling heavy guns. It carried four riders and could go up to 9kph.

He built another at the Pen-y-Darren ironworks in South Wales in 1804. This could pull much greater loads than a horse, and at a steady 8 kph. Trevithick's engines used high-pressure steam. This had far more power than the earlier **atmospheric** (Newcomen) or low-pressure (Watt) engines used to pump out mines or drive machinery.

Trevithick left his experiments to go to South America, where he hoped to make a fortune by using steam engines to re-open old Spanish silver mines. By the time he got back other inventors had taken the lead in building locomotives in Britain and he died poor and forgotten.

Trevithick demonstrated his 'Catch-me-who-can' locomotive in London in 1809. One of the onlookers was George Stephenson.

Rack railways

It was widely believed that smooth iron wheels would not be able to grip smooth iron rails. Trevithick's locomotives showed that this was not so. This did not stop other inventors trying different systems. Mines inspector John Blenkinsop invented a locomotive with toothed wheels and rails at Middleton colliery in Yorkshire. This became the forerunner of the rack railways used on steep gradients in mountainous areas the world over.

The Stephensons

George Stephenson (1781–1848)

George Stephenson was born in Killingworth, near Newcastle, into a poor family. He only learned to read when he was eighteen and taught himself about machinery by mending clocks. He also invented a safety lamp for coal miners which would not set off explosive gases.

Stephenson's first **locomotives** were for hauling coal along local wagon ways. In 1820–1822 he laid out a 13 km railway linking Hetton colliery in County Durham to the River Wear. He next engineered the Stockton and Darlington Railway. This was opened in 1825 and was the first public line using locomotives. In practice it only hauled **freight**. Passengers were pulled along the rails in horse-drawn carriages.

Stephenson's greatest project was the Liverpool and Manchester Railway, opened in 1830, for which he surveyed the route and supervised the construction. It was such a great technical and financial success, it sparked off '**railway mania**'. By 1850, Britain's major cities were linked to one another by railways on which trains were travelling regularly at up to 80 kph.

George Stephenson's Locomotion No. 1, built for the Stockton and Darlington railway. There were no cabs on locomotives to shelter the driver and fireman until the 1850s.

The Rainhill Trials

The contract for the Liverpool and Manchester line's locomotives depended on success in a competition held over a week in October 1829, at Rainhill, near Liverpool. The three competitors were required to cover at least 133 km in a day, at an average speed of not less than 16 kph, over a 3 km course. Stephenson's *Rocket* covered 19 km in 53 minutes on its first run. He won the £500 prize and the contract for the line.

Robert Stephenson (1803–1859)

Robert Stephenson benefited not only from a practical apprenticeship with his father, but also from a spell at Edinburgh University, and time as a mining engineer in Colombia.

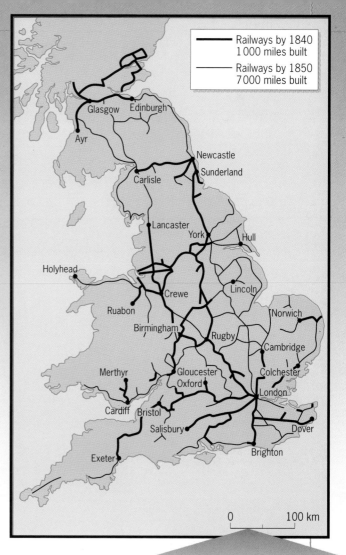

Britain's railway system in 1840 and in 1850

He headed the world's first locomotive manufacturing works, founded in Newcastle-Upon-Tyne in 1823, and ten years later became chief engineer of the London to Birmingham Railway.

His later Newcastle to Berwick line involved a six-arch iron bridge over the Tyne, for which he used Nasmyth's newly-invented steam-hammer to drive the foundations. Robert Stephenson's greatest triumphs were a tubular bridge linking Anglesey to the Welsh mainland across the Menai Straits and another crossing Canada's St Lawrence river at Montreal.

So steam not only powered trains and machinery, it also helped build the bridges which transformed the landscape.

Steam challenges sail

EARLY EXPERIMENTS

1690 – People like Denis Papin had suggested that ships might be powered by steam.

1696 – Thomas Savery patented a design for a ship with paddle-wheels.

1788 – William Symington combines steam-power and paddle-wheels successfully.

1802 – William Symington built the tug *Charlotte Dundas* which was used to tow barges on canals.

1807 – American Robert Fulton's *Clermont* made the first long-distance journey by steam, from New York to Albany and back, some 300 miles.

1812 – Fulton began a steam ferry service between New York and Jersey City. Soon steam passenger services began in Britain on the Clyde, Mersey and Thames rivers.

Passengers, mail or cargo?

By the 1820s, steamships were being used on inland and coastal waters to provide regular services which, unlike sailing ships, did not depend on the wind and the tides. A London–Paris service began in 1821. But the early steamers needed so much space for fuel that they could carry little bulky cargo and relied instead on the higher returns from carrying passengers and mail. In 1838, three crossings of the Atlantic were at last made entirely under steam-power and regular transatlantic services began.

The *Charlotte Dundas* on the Forth and Clyde canal.

Brunel's firsts

In 1845, Isambard Kingdom Brunel's *Great Britain* became the first iron steamer driven by a **screw-propeller** rather than paddles, to cross the Atlantic, carrying 60 passengers and 600 tons of cargo in 14 days. It is now in dry dock at Bristol, where it can be visited.

Launched in 1858 Brunel's *Great Eastern*, at 211 metres and 18,914 tons, was by far the biggest ship ever built to date. It had room for 12,000 tons of coal and 4000 passengers, and was intended to be able to go round the world without refuelling. The *Great Eastern* proved to be too expensive to run, but it did lay the first transatlantic telegraph cable in 1865–66 before being broken up.

Isambard Kingdom Brunel (1806–59), the greatest engineer of his day, poses by the giant chains used for launching the *Great Eastern*. Brunel also built the Great Western Railway from London to Bristol and designed the spectular Clifton Suspension Bridge at Bristol.

Steam steams ahead!

Improvements in engine design in the 1860s meant steamers needed far less fuel, leaving more room for bulky cargoes. Wheat and timber from North America, and meat and wool from Australia could now be sent cheaply to Europe. So steam bought increased trade to all these areas. By 1865, more steamers than sailing ships were being built in Britain. At the same time the navies of many countries finally began to abandon wooden sailing ships in favour of iron (later steel) ones, powered by steam. By 1907, liners were crossing the Atlantic in just five days.

Railway revolutions

Building railways created jobs for hundreds of thousands of labourers and craftsmen, as well as a huge demand for bricks, timber, iron and glass, thus boosting the industries which produced these materials.

The boost to industry

The 3 km long Box Tunnel, built by Brunel on the Great Western Railway, took 4000 men and 300 horses 2 years to build. It used 30,000,000 bricks, plus a ton of gunpowder and a ton of candles every week. The short section of the railway between Bath and Bristol alone needed another two viaducts, four bridges and seven tunnels.

Railways round the world

British engineers and craftsmen helped to build the first railways in Europe – in Belgium, France and Germany. By 1848, Berlin, in Germany, was linked by rail with the Baltic Sea to the north, with the coal mines of Silesia to the east, and with the industries of the Ruhr to the west. By 1850, all Belgium's main towns were linked by rail.

Excavating the Camden cutting for Robert Stephenson's London to Birmingham Railway. Construction consumed vast quantities of bricks, timber, stone and iron.

In North America major new cities, like Atlanta and Winnipeg, grew up as railway junctions. In 1830, Chicago had 50 people and more pigs than houses. By 1900, it was a city of a million people and the centre for a new mail-order industry, which could not have existed before the coming of the railway age.

More important still, railways opened up vast new areas for farming in North America, Australia and Argentina.

Steam-powered ships could bring wheat, canned fruit or fish and, from the 1880s, refrigerated meat, right round the world so cheaply that only the most efficient British farmers could compete, and many switched to producing milk or vegetables instead.

By 1900, the daily breakfast-table – with bacon from Denmark, tea from India and sugar from the West Indies – provided British schoolchildren with a practical demonstration of the workings of international trade.

Thomas Lipton's grocery empire included tea plantations in Ceylon (Sri Lanka). Notice the **locomotive**, and the ship which has a funnel for its steam engine, as well as sails.

Railways go to war

Governments soon realized that railways could be used to transport troops and **artillery** swiftly to put down riots or rebellions. During the American Civil War (1861–5) railways played a major role in keeping the huge armies supplied and fed. Generals gave high priority to the defence and capture of key lines and junctions. Prussia's victory over France in 1870-1, owed much to the skilful use of railways to move troops swiftly, without long, tiring marches, and then being able to concentrate them in large numbers ready to do battle.

More railway revolutions

DISTANCES SHRINK

By making transport so much faster and cheaper, railways helped to bring the different parts of Britain closer together:

• newspapers printed in a few big cities, could be delivered everywhere by overnight trains

• manufactured goods were distributed nationwide

• national brands of household goods, medicines and canned and non-perishable foods, (such as sugar, tea, cocoa or syrup) began to appear

• pre-stamped postage was introduced charging for weight only, regardless of distance

• fresh fish, packed into ice at Hull, Fleetwood or Yarmouth, was sent swiftly to big, inland cities

• fish-and-chips became a national dish by the 1860s.

When tourism began, Thomas Cook, a Baptist preacher, organized an outing for 500 people to hear a lecture against drinking. He went on to build up a worldwide travel agency, based on railways and ships.

Travelling for pleasure

Before railways, travelling was tiring, uncomfortable, and sometimes dangerous. Railways offered fast, safe, reliable travel in relative comfort, all year round. It was also cheaper than going by road. Special railway excursions began in the 1830s, usually as church or company outings. As railways spread over Europe, foreign travel became affordable to the middle classes. Queen Victoria's visits to the remote Scottish Highlands made them a popular destination. Seaside towns, such as Blackpool, Scarborough, Bournemouth and Cromer became busy holiday resorts.

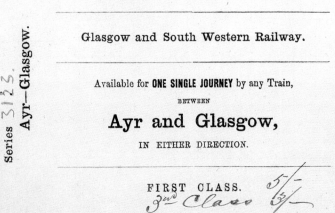

No.

COOK'S BRITISH TOURS.

Glasgow and South Western Railway.

Available for **ONE SINGLE JOURNEY** by any Train,

BETWEEN

Ayr and Glasgow,

IN EITHER DIRECTION.

FIRST CLASS. 5/-

3ᵈ Class 5/

Series 3132. Ayr—Glasgow.

In America, George Pullman made long distance travel bearable by developing luxury railway coaches with fold-away beds and dining-cars with kitchens. Luxury hotels were built where main railway lines terminated.

The impact on towns

The first railways were built to benefit industry. They mainly moved goods, not people. So after a train left the London, Paddington **terminus** of Brunel's Great Western Railway, its first stop was Slough, 20 km away.

Later, carrying passengers became more important. Railways transported people within large cities between stations built every few miles. Railways also made daily commuting possible. City of London bankers could live in the Thames Valley or along the south coast, and Manchester merchants out in leafy Cheshire.

Early passengers on the world's first underground railway, opened in London in 1863.

A number of towns became important as railway junctions and centres for the repair and manufacture of **locomotives**. These include Crewe, Rugby, York, Swindon, and Stratford in East London.

Finally, by cutting the costs of transporting bricks from Bedford or Peterborough and roofing-slates from Wales, railways helped to make many towns look more like one another than when builders could only afford to use local building materials. Steam power helped to change not only where people lived, but also what their houses looked like.

Steam at your service

Industry

After textiles and mining, the most important industry to be affected by steam power was engineering. Steam power made it possible to create more powerful and accurate machine-tools – machines that made parts for making other machines. These included devices for cutting, grinding, planing and punching holes in metal.

Steam-powered machinery was also developed for mass production – producing huge quantities of items at ever lower prices. Through the power of steam, small metal objects, such as pins, nails, screws, cog-wheels, keys, hand tools, buttons, buckles, pen-nibs and coins, became much cheaper.

Nasmyth's steam-hammer as sketched in his notebook. The basic design took him just half an hour.

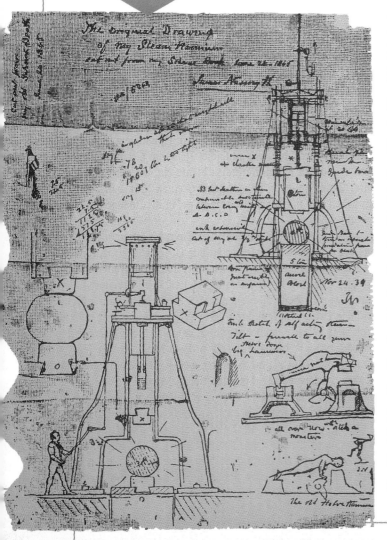

Engineering

In 1839, English engineer James Nasmyth (1808–90) invented a gigantic steam-hammer which was used for forging parts of Brunel's revolutionary all-iron steamship *Great Britain*. The hammer part of it was raised by steam power and fell by the force of gravity. In 1845, Nasmyth adapted it to become a pile-driver for sinking **piles** on which bridges could be built. A pile that would have taken twelve hours to drive by previous methods could now be driven into position in four minutes. Steam-powered dredgers were invented for excavating docks and harbours.

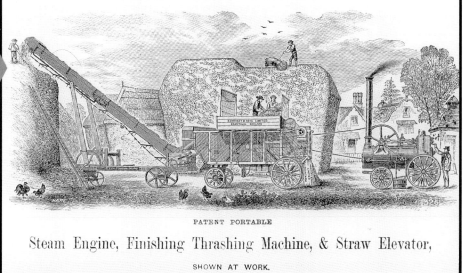

R. HORNSBY & SONS, LIMITED,
SPITTLEGATE IRON WORKS, GRANTHAM.

PATENT PORTABLE
Steam Engine, Finishing Thrashing Machine, & Straw Elevator,
SHOWN AT WORK.

A portable steam engine powers a threshing-machine and conveyor belt.

Farming

Steam-powered pumps also affected the landscape in other ways. First developed for use in mines, they were easily adapted for draining marshy land, like the Fens of eastern England. In 1842, Ransome's, a firm based in Ipswich, Suffolk, which specialized in agricultural machinery, invented a steam-powered machine for threshing crops to separate out the grain. They launched a steam-powered plough in 1854. Steam ploughs were, however, very expensive and only used by rich farmers with big fields. But many farms installed fixed steam engines which powered other machines for crushing or pulping root crops into fodder, chopping up straw, or sawing wood. The steam could also be drawn off to heat rooms where crops were dried out.

Mr Maudslay's marvellous machines

In 1802, Henry Maudslay made a set of 43 machines to manufacture **pulley**-blocks for the Royal Navy. They were designed by Marc Brunel, father of Isambard Kingdom Brunel. Previously this task had employed 110 skilled craftsmen. The new machines, installed in Portsmouth dockyard, needed only 10 unskilled labourers to operate them and produced 130,000 blocks a year. Power came from a 30-horsepower steam engine. Some of the machines were still in use a century after Maudslay's death in 1831.

25

The turbine

Power from falling water

In 1827, Frenchman Benoit Fourneyron designed a **turbine**. Water poured down an upright pipe with angled **vanes** inside it. These made the water swirl so that when it reached more angled vanes, mounted on an axle, it made the axle revolve, driving machinery attached to it. Fourneyron engines worked well where vertical flows of water came from mountain streams or waterfalls. By 1843, they were working in 129 factories across Europe and Mexico.

In 1873, the largest Fourneyron turbine ever was built at Sweetapple's paper-mill near Godalming, Surrey. In 1881, Godalming installed the first **hydroelectric** power station, using the River Wey's flow to light local streets. The world's first large hydroelectric power station opened at Niagara Falls, New York State, in 1895. Nowadays a quarter of the world's electricity is produced by water-driven turbines.

Steam turbines

In 1884, English engineer Charles Parsons invented a turbine using high-pressure steam, flowing through a series of fixed and rotating vanes, to generate rapid rotary (circular) motion which could power a generator to produce electricity.

How a turbine works

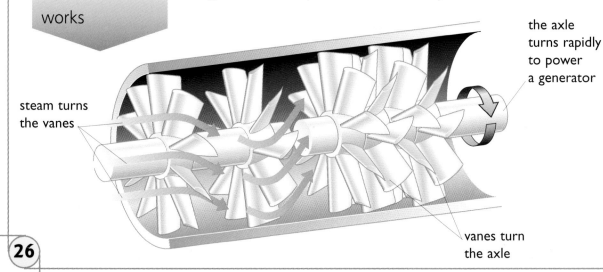

the axle turns rapidly to power a generator

steam turns the vanes

vanes turn the axle

Charles Parson's revolutionary high-speed *Turbinia*

By 1888, Parsons turbines were in use in American power stations. They became the most common way to generate electric power.

In 1894, Parsons built a fast launch, *Turbinia*, to prove that turbines could be used to power ships. The Royal Navy showed no interest until in 1897, at a huge fleet review to mark Queen Victoria's Diamond Jubilee, Parsons sailed *Turbinia* right through the assembled ships at the unheard of speed of 34.5 knots – 25 per cent faster than the destroyers sent to chase it! The Navy's first turbine ship, the destroyer *Viper*, was launched in 1900.

Look – no hands!

In 1510, Italian artist Leonardo da Vinci illustrated a simple turbine in action – the kitchen chimney-jack, a fan on a spindle mounted above an open cooking-fire. Hot air currents rising from the fire turned the fan as they passed through it, thus rotating the spindle which, by a chain-link, turned a spit so that the meat was evenly roasted.

The fossil fuel age

Energy from the earth

Before the invention of steam power the sources of energy needed for agriculture, industry, mining and transportation were either unreliable – such as wind and water-power – or, in the case of human and animal muscle-power, of limited strength. Steam technology made it possible, by using coal, to unlock an energy source stored up over millions of years. Steam engines did not need feeding like horses and people. They ran on coal which was dug out of the ground. At first it must have seemed as if supplies of coal – and therefore energy – were limitless.

Making the impossible possible

By 1870, Britain's mines, railways and factories were equipped with steam engines that could develop 4,000,000 horsepower – about the same as the muscle energy of 40,000,000 fit adult men. 40,000,000 men would have been a third more than the entire population of the British Isles – men, women and children. To have fed them would have needed three times as much wheat as Britain produced each year. And even if 40,000,000 men had been able to live on wheat alone and work without ever resting or sleeping, they could never have been organized to push trains at 100 kph or turn 50,000 spindles at a time. In other words, the modern world of factories, railways and steamships could never have developed as it did.

This Watt engine, installed in 1777, pumped water for the Birmingham Canal until the 1890s, when it was finally demolished.

King coal

As coal became the key source of energy in the steam age, industry became concentrated on coalfields – in South Yorkshire, Lancashire and the West Midlands, in the Scottish Lowlands and South Wales and on Tyneside. Where coal was mined, iron and steel were made, ships built, guns forged and cloth woven. By 1913, coal accounted for a tenth of Britain's exports, and mining and transporting it employed almost a million men.

Wearmouth Colliery 1879. Tall chimneys and the wheels of winding-gear show the importance of steam engines. Horses are still used to haul smaller waggons.

Steam surpassed

In 1925, coal-rich Britain still relied on steam to produce 90 per cent of its energy needs. Switzerland, by contrast lacked coal, but being mountainous could produce electricity cheaply through water-driven **turbines**. There steam accounted for only 6 per cent of energy needs.

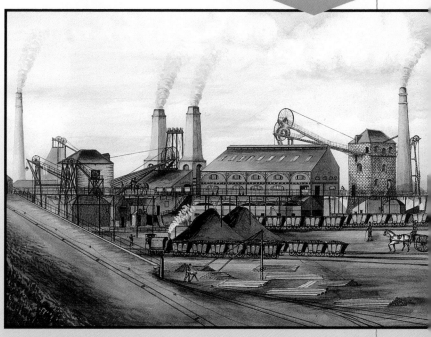

In Britain, oil, electricity, diesel and nuclear power have all reduced the importance of steam power in the twentieth century. But it remains important, especially for railways, in many developing countries, such as India and China.

Without steam power, however, there would have been no **Industrial Revolution** – the 'revolution' or change in how goods were produced. It brought change to nearly every aspect of people's lives, made Britain a world economic leader and brought about the modern world.

Time-line

1654	Guericke exhibits the force of **atmospheric presure**
1690	Papin shows that steam can drive a piston
1698	Savery patents a steam-powered pump for use in mines
1712	Newcomen's atmospheric engine is installed at a colliery near Dudley, Staffordshire.
1728	Iron rails used in Cumberland
1770	Cugnot makes a steam-powered carriage to pull **artillery**
1777	First Watt engine installed in a cornish mine
1782	Watt designs a system to produce rotary motion
1802	Brunel designs steam-powered block-making machines for Portsmouth dockyard
1803	Trevithick builds the first **locomotive**. Surrey Iron Railway opened
1807	Fulton's *Clermont* shows steamships can travel long distances
1814	Stephenson builds his first locomotive. *The Times* newspaper is the first in the world to be printed by steam
1823	The Stephensons open the world's first locomotive factory in Newcastle-Upon-Tyne
1827	Fourneyron invents the water-powered **turbine**
1829	Stephenson's *Rocket* wins the Rainhill trials
1830	Liverpool and Manchester Railway opened
1838	I. K. Brunel's *Great Western* is the first steamship to cross the Atlantic regularly
1839	Nasmyth invents the steam hammer
1841	Thomas Cook organizes the first railway excursion
1860	Royal Navy launches its first steam-powered ironclad warship, HMS *Warrior*
1879	Von Siemens exhibits the first electric train
1884	Parsons patents the steam turbine
1894	Turbine-powered *Turbinia* is launched
1895	The world's first large-scale hydro-electric power plant is opened at Niagara Falls

Glossary

artillery   heavy guns used in fighting on land

atmospheric pressure   the weight of air from the top of the atmosphere pressing on layers of earth below

capstan   thick revolving cylinder that often has cable or rope around it

condensed   when water is heated it becomes vapour (steam) and when this cools it returns to being water

cylinder   hollow container with straight sides and circular ends

exports   goods sent abroad from one country for sale in another country

freight   transportation of goods, often in containers, usually by water or air

horsepower   unit for measuring the power of an engine. One horsepower = about 750 watts

hydroelectric   using the power of water to generate electricity

immigrant   person who has come from another country

impressions   identical reprints from a printing plate

Industrial Revolution   the introduction and spread of machines to do work that was previously done by hand

locomotive   an engine that has sufficient power to move itself along and to pull a load, usually means a train engine

mass production   the production of large numbers of identical goods by machine

patent   legal document protecting the right of an inventor to sole use of his invention for a period of years; anyone else wishing to copy it has to pay

piles   heavy beams driven vertically into the ground as a support for a bridge

piston   sliding cylinder which moves up and down inside a close-fitting tube

pulley   grooved wheel for cord to pass over, set in a block, and used for changing the direction of a force; can also be a wheel or drum fixed on a shaft and turned by a belt

railway mania   period of rapid expansion of the railway network (1830s–40s)

royalty   money paid for the use of something patented or owned by someone else

screw-propeller   revolving shaft with blades for propelling ships or aircraft

terminus   station at the end of a railway or bus route

turbine   rotary motor driven by the flow of water or gas

vacuum   space from which air has been removed

vane   blade of screw propeller or windmill

watt   unit of power (one joule per second)

Index